The Bold and Brave Soldier

Written by:

Daniel Kirschler

www.beefriendsomebody.com

Copyright © 2017 Daniel Kirschler
All rights reserved.
ISBN-10: 1979095159
ISBN-13: 978-1979095150

John 3:17

Not that long ago, in a
world so big, but small.

Men and women, from
nation to nation, received
a life changing call.

BeeFriend

Somebody

It wasn't a call from Mom.
And it wasn't a call from
Dad.

It didn't make them
happy.
But it didn't make them
mad.

BeeFriend

Somebody

The truth of the matter,
and it doesn't seem right.

BeeFriend

Somebody

Sometimes people get together just to pick a fight.

It wasn't a fight about
potato chips, or who gets
the last ice cream.

BeeFriend

Somebody

It wasn't a fight about
video games, or the
beloved hometown team.

BeeFriend 

Somebody

No, this was a fight
fought with all their might.

BeeFriend

Somebody

It wasn't a fight about
video games, or the
beloved hometown team.

No, this was a fight
fought with all their might.

BeeFriend

Somebody

For honor and for country
and for what they thought
was right.

BeeFriend

Somebody

If not for their bravery -
both near and far away.

BeeFriend 

Somebody

The world would be a
whole lot different than
the world we know today.

We can't forget about
those who served, even
to this day.

BeeFriend

Somebody

Giving us the freedom
and safety to go outside
and play.

This might be a little too intense for someone at your age.

BeeFriend

Somebody

But trust me, friend, you'll understand one day, why I wrote what is on this page.

Hopefully then - not too
long from now - when
you're just a little bit
older.

You will understand what
this means, and why I
love, each and every bold
and brave soldier.

BeeFriend

Somebody

www.beefriendsomebody.com

www.ingramcontent.com/pod-product-compliance
Lightning Source LLC
Chambersburg PA
CBHW061930270726
48660CB00003BA/1128